Sweet Hour of Prayer
THE ANSWERED PRAYERS

**Compiled, edited & written by
Phillip Wells**

XULON PRESS

Xulon Press
2301 Lucien Way #415
Maitland, FL 32751
407.339.4217
www.xulonpress.com

Unless otherwise indicated, Scripture quotations taken from the King James Version (KJV) – *public domain*.

Printed in the United States of America.

ISBN-13: 978-1-6312-9637-6

Sweet Hour of Prayer

Table of Contents

Introduction ix
My Mother's Prayer 1
Sweet Hour of Prayer 2
The Lord's Prayer 3
Your Morning Prayer 4
Uncle Pete 6
Answered prayer 10
The Devil and Aquilla 13
Max – Answered prayers 19
His Way 24
The flood 26
Haiti–traffic court 28
Chilean miners 30
The Man Who Thanked the Sea Gulls- 32
It is well with my Soul 35
Witnessing a miracle! 37
Another Room 39
Moldova 41
Irene 43
Mission trip to Moldova 44
GOD'S "PHONE" NUMBER 46
Pump priming 50
Ben, Just Checking In 52
A Visit from a friend 55
Four Boy friends 56

The Attorney 59

A Cup of Coffee 61

The Big Wheel 63

God, Save us! 67

Unanswered prayers 69

WHAT HAPPENS IN HEAVEN WHEN WE PRAY? 71

Victory, God's way 73

Across the river 74

On to Ai. 77

Visitors from a far country 79

First day of the week. 81

A Father, a Daughter and a Dog 82

A little child will lead us 87

Out of the mouths of babes! 90

Kids will be kids 92

Introduction

We know, or should know, Prayer is the most powerful and important event in which we can engage. We are commanded by Jesus to pray without ceasing. This booklet cites some events that illustrate this power.

Many of the events cited were actual occurrences as witnessed and reported by knowledgeable individuals. Some are reprinted from email messages carrying an important message.

Others are reprinted from comments made by young children. As Art Linkletter used to say, "Kids say the darnedest things.

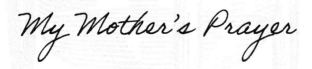

My Mother's Prayer

I never can forget the day I heard my mother kindly say "You're leaving now my tender care; Remember, child your mother's prayer."

When-ever I think of her so dear, I feel her angel spirit near: A voice comes floating on the air, reminding me of Mother's prayer

I never can forget the voice that always made my heart rejoice: Tho' I have wandered God knows where. Still I remember mother's prayer

Tho' years have gone, I can't forget those words of love I hear them yet: I see her by the old arm chair. My mother dear, in humble prayer.

I never can forget the hour I felt the Savior's cleansing power: My sin and guilt He cancelled there, t'was there He answered, Mother's prayer.

Oh, praise the Lord for saving grace! We'll meet up yonder face to face, the home above together share. In answer to my mother's prayer.

Sweet Hour of Prayer

Authors: William Walford, William Bradvury

Sweet Hour of prayer! Sweet hour of prayer! That calls me from a world of care.

And bids me at my Father's throne make all my wants and wises known;

In seasons of distress and grief, my soul has often found relief

And oft escaped the tempter's snare by thy return, sweet hour of prayer

Sweet hour of prayer! Sweet hour of prayer! Thy wings shall my petition bear

To Him whose truth and faithfulness engage the waiting soul to bless;

And since He bids me seek His face, believe His work and trust His grace,

I'll cast on Him my every care, and wait for thee, sweet hour of prayer.

Sweet hour of prayer! Sweet hour of prayer! May I thy consolation share.

Till from Mount Pisgah's lofty height, I view my home, and take my flight:

This robe of flesh I'll drop, and rise to seize the everlasting prize;

And shout, while passing through the air, farewell, farewell, sweet hour of prayer.

The Lord's Prayer

Luke 11: 2-4

O ne of His disciples said unto him, "Lord, teach us to pray..."
And He said unto them," when ye pray, say,
Our Father, who art in Heaven, Hallowed be thy name.
Thy kingdom come.
Thy will be done, as in Heaven, so in earth.
Give us day by day our daily bread.
And forgive us our sins; for we also forgive everyone that is indebted
to us. And lead us not into temptation; but deliver us from evil."
   Amen

3

Your Morning Prayer

Y ou never know when God is going to bless you!
  Good things happen when you least expect them!
Dear Lord, I thank You for this day,

Thank You for my being able to see and hear this morning. I'm blessed because You are a forgiving God and an understanding God. You have done so much for me and You keep on blessing me. Forgive me this day for everything I have done, said or thought that was not pleasing to you.

I ask now for Your forgiveness, Please keep me safe from all danger and harm. Help me to start this day with a new attitude and plenty of gratitude. Let me make the best of each and every day, to clear my mind so that I can hear from You. Please broaden my mind that I can accept all things. Let me not whine and whimper over things I have no control over. And give me the best response when I'm pushed beyond my limits. .1 know that when I can't pray, you listen to my heart. Continue to use me to do Your will. Continue to bless me that I may be a blessing to others.

Keep me strong that I may help the weak. Keep me uplifted that I may have words of encouragement for others. I pray for those that are lost and can't find their way, I pray for those that are misjudged and misunderstood. I pray for those who don't know You intimately, for those that will, not share it with others 1 pray for those that don't believe. But I thank You that I believe that God changes people and God changes things. I pray for all my sisters

4

and brothers. For each and every family member in Their house-holds. I pray for peace, love and joy in their homes that they are out of debt and all their needs are met. I pray that every eye that reads this knows there is no problem, circumstance, or situation greater than God. Every battle is in Your hands for You to fight.

I pray that these words be received into the hearts of every eye that sees it. In **Jesus' name. Amen!**

Uncle Pete

Truth is stranger than fiction, especially when the impossible happens.

Thanksgiving, to the family, it's a prelude to Christmas, especially for the kids. When they gathered around the dining room table for the traditional Thanksgiving dinner, they were all kids, we were all kids; at least all of us acted like it, Who was going to get the drum sticks, four were arguing about and over them, the problem was there was only two drumsticks. It appears there would be a fight until Uncle Pete stepped in the middle of the argument, he settled the problem. Easy he said, he would take one and Aunt Susan would get the second one. "No problem, now everyone is happy." Well not quite everyone, the kids weren't.

With the drumstick problem solved, the immediate question was white or dark meat, then pass the sweet potatoes, green beans, rolls and the cranberry sauce. Everyone, all sixteen of them settled down to eat, there was no time to argue and fight, they were too busy eating to argue, they were almost too busy eating to talk, but, the usual family kind of talk filtered through. Who got married since last Thanksgiving?

That was the last time all of them gathered together. Who is getting a divorce? Who's having a baby and who has had a baby since last year? It seems the whole family is fertile so there's always a bunch of babies. Most everyone ooh'd and aw'd as the pictures were passed round the table. That is everyone except Uncle Pete.

6

Everyone knew he just wasn't a baby kind of guy; he wanted no part of the baby brigade, and let it be known. "Don't want to see no picture of those kids, just keep those pictures, don't need to see them, don't want to see them. Babies are just too much trouble. Not only that. But they smell funny."

It was unusual, Uncle Pete usually was the last one to leave the table, at least if there was a piece of pumpkin or mincemeat pie left. Whipped cream on the pumpkin pie, none on the mincemeat. "Don't want to ruin it with that stuff." "Got a tingling in my left arm, don't feel too good, nothing too serious, just need to get up and move around a little." Scooted the chair back stumble a little as he did.

Ruth reached out to help, "Don't need no help. I'll get by without any help. I'll just sit on the couch and watch the Cowboys' football game, got to have someone to cheer against." That started it; they all choose sides as they decided who they would cheer for or against, except the four that decided to move to the den to watch a different game.

"Come on Uncle Pete, you don't seem to be getting into the game, what's the matter?"

"Don't rightly know, just don't feel right, don't rightly think I've ever felt this bad before. Got this tingling in my arm. My chest feels like Randle backed up his truck and parked it on my chest, can't hardly breathe. I think I just need to lay down for a few minutes."

"Hey Ruth, Uncle Pete needs to lay down, that OK with you?"

"Why sure, just move those coats off' a the bed and he can lay down there."

"Stumble just getting up he did," replied George, "grab hold an hep him a little."

"Don't need no help from you or any body else, I can make it on my own. Always have, always will. Now leave me be and just get out'a the way and let me be."

7

Before the doorway to the bed room was reached, Uncle Pete was on the floor, just twitching and kind'a foaming at the mouth. No body knew what to do; at least they didn't for a while.. Then someone yelled, "Call a doctor, call an ambulance, call 911 do something." Uncle Pete was helped to the bed, carried would be a better term for it.

Hours passed; at least it seemed like hours, in reality only minutes, the ambulance was there followed by a police car. All were stressed except the medical people; they appeared as if it was business as usual. In reality, it probably was for them.

Pete had long since ceased to be alert; he did kind of twitch once in a while, nothing more. That cuff around his arm didn't work; at least the medical guy said something like that and did it again. The tall thin guy working with the cuff wrinkled his forehead muttered, he don't look good, he needs to be in the hospital. He said this as the ambulance stopped out in front, sirens blaring and all those light flashing, it was a sight.

No one seemed to know who called the doctor, but Dr. Melenkamp waited in the Emergency Room as the ambulance arrived. Pete was rushed directly to an examination room, then to ICU. It was thought that move was strange, the doctor had not more than glanced at him, never the less; he was on his way and would remain there for four days, progressively getting worse. Discharged to a nursing home for a few days then to home with hospice care.

A stroke, at least that's what the doctor said was the problem, left him blind, those old eyes just looked dead, guess they was, deaf and without the benefit of speech. Practically dead, at least that's the way he looked. He remained that way for months, getting no worse nor any better either for that matter.

That was then this is now, almost exactly a year to the day since the family's last get together. The talk settled around Uncle Pete's condition.

Dr. Melenkamp followed the progress, or rather the lack of any. Doc followed Pete's condition daily, almost hour by hour. Around the first of November he had announced, "He's going fast, he can't make it more than a few days. I'll be back tomorrow to see how he's doing."

The entire family was present; hovering around the bed, if one didn't know better, an outsider would have reckoned they looked and acted like vultures. After all, the doctor had told them of the near eventual demise of Uncle Pete. Susan had to be told, that meant he was a going'a die any minute. Out of respect they wanted to be present, one never knows, they may be remembered in the will. No one knew for sure but it was suspected he had a tidy sum stashed somewhere.

They wanted to get in on it if there was any. Everyone was there, just then the doctor walked in to see how the patient was doing, Uncle Pete immediately sat up in bed, looked around with previously sightless eyes, spoke to Susan, Ruth, Ruby, George, calling them by name, acknowledged everyone, said he was hungry, promptly fell backward dead.

Dr. Melenkamp reckoned that couldn't of happened, couldn't see without eyes, and hadn't had any since the spell a year ago. Couldn't hear, being deaf for the better part of a year, couldn't speak, being dumb since last Thanksgiving. Never the less, he had to admit he saw and heard everything and still couldn't believe it.

Answered prayer

Hunting was a way of life for Jerry, an enjoyable way, especially rabbit hunting. Of course, when other forms of game were in season, they were the favorite. That would also include deer and duck hunting. When the mood struck there was fishing, especially trout fishing on the first day of March, it was important to be at the creek bank at daybreak. When none of these were present, there was always golf. Some times although not often, Mary, the "best wife" as he referred to her accompanied, when she wasn't along, there was best friend Paul. It was highly unusual for the three of them to be together at a time such as this.

A much anticipated opening day of rabbit hunting season found Jerry and Paul heading to the field, a field owned by Burt who was more than happy to permit Jerry and Paul to hunt. They were responsible people; some times Burt would join them. Today was not one of those days. Daylight peaked over the far line of trees, the car slowed, eased into the parking area generally utilized for that purpose. Today was a crisp, clear day, ideal for hunting. Rabbits should be moving; certainly Sparky was more than ready. Sometimes quails are flushed in this area, won't do any good, they're out of season. Not only that, but Sparky likes to chase them, that messes him up when he should be concentrating on rabbits.

Within a few hundred yards, a chain link fence spread across the entire field. It was there but was not a concern, it had always been there. It was just a matter of climbing over. Jerry steadied the fence, pulled the top down, Paul crossed over. Following Paul's crossing, he repaid the favor; it was Jerry's turn. Neither gave the activity much attention, it was an activity they had accomplished hundreds of times over the years; after all, it wasn't even considered an inconvenience.

Stepping over, Jerry's foot caught on the top strain, he fell clutching his favorite unloaded shotgun. It was always unloaded, unloaded with the safety on, he was careful that way, after all, someone could get seriously hurt. The butt end of the gun struck the ground, the unloaded gun discharged with the pellets striking Jerry in the chest and stomach. Avalanche of blood covered the area. Jerry lay on the ground not moving. Paul had no idea what to do, having never experienced anything close the events taking place.

The fun day immediately became a crisis. "How will we get help?" Paul was not sure he said the words but he certainly though them, they were a long way from help and no way to summon any. Help was needed, and needed immediately. The only thing to be done was to carry Jerry to the car. It was accomplished. Later, Paul acknowledged he had no idea how the feat was done, Jerry was as large as Paul and weighted as much.

Immediately after delivering Jerry to the emergency room, Paul contacted the Church's Pastor advising him of the situation. The Church's prayer warriors as they were called immediately sprung into action. As was there wont, each calling the others until the task had been completed. The word spread, "Jerry was in the hospital with a serious life threatening hunting accident, pray that he may live." Fourteen ladies sprang into action, each stopped what they were doing and prayed, and pray they did, their unofficial title "Prayer Warriors" was well founded.

The small Church was called into a special prayer meeting to pray for Jerry, praying that he may not die. Days passed, as did weeks and months. Jerry lived, but just barely, the doctor continued to advise them that prayer was the only thing keeping Jerry alive. There had been no improvement in his condition since he was brought to the hospital.

The family consulted their Pastor for advise, not knowing what should be done, their prayers were being answered, but there did not seemed to be improvement in Jerry's condition. Pastor Brooks was asked if perhaps the Church was praying for the wrong end, suggesting that perhaps their prayer should be that "God's will be done." The prayer request immediately became as the Pastor recommended. Within mere hours, Jerry breathed his last, the prayer was answered at last, and "God's will" was done.

The first prayer was answered even though it was not in the will of God. When the prayer was changed, the new prayer was also answered.

The Devil and Aquilla

T hink of a Southern gentleman, any Southern Gentleman especially an elderly one~ Surely a soft spoken, sincere, honest and
hardworking man came to mind. That described Aquilla. In his
younger days, he stood tall and thin; due to a life style that included
hard work, temperate and prudence in everything. If one looked the
definition of "religious" in the dictionary, one would probably see
the image of Aquilla; he was that type of person, highly respected
by all. Now, the years have caught up with him, something that
happens to all of us who are fortunate to reach a good old age, he
wasn't quite as tall and straight as he was once, Other than that, his
life style had not changed.

However, his hearing that at one time ranked with the best,
was now non existent. Compensation was made via a hearing horn
held firmly in place so as to hear whatever there was to hear. Any
way, that's what he thought, actually there was a lot of missed
conversation.

As was his wont, late Saturday afternoons mid winter found
him sitting around the pot bellied stove at the local grocery store
with friends. As usual, no customers were present; at least no customers, who were there to buy, seven men were present on this date.
With little or nothing to do, all were busy mostly swapping yarns.
No one ever questioned if the stories were true; it was assumed
they were not.

Silas bent over asking Aquilla, "Why do you go to Church every Sunday, you know you can't hear anything the Preacher says?' There was no reaction. Aquilla had heard nothing. Silas restated the question, with no response, others joined in, and it was great fun for all, and still no response. Everyone was enjoying the action, at some level; they were making fun of Aquilla and in what they considered a good nature ribbing. Someone grabbed a piece of paper and scribbled a note asking the same question, "why do you go to Church every Sunday", this time they reminded Aquilla with an added reminder that they all knew he couldn't hear.

Aquilla never missed a beat, responding to the question, he noted with the response, "just want the Devil to know what side I'm on." He was that kind of man.

There were no other questions.

midmorning on the fourth day. As he was putting

Uncle Wayne

Uncle Wayne was one of a kind, we know lots of people are defined in that (Insert Image_1)manner, but Uncle Wayne was special. He was Uncle Wayne to all of those who knew him, and anyone who met him knew him.

Many, maybe most who served in the Military service during the Second World War and all wars, often don't talk about their war time experiences. We suspect that is the case in all wars, the term "War is hell" is accurate and understandable. There was one episode, which Uncle Wayne shared, and then only one time. Other than not wanting to recall his war experiences, we suspect he was of the opinion no one believed him. Those of us who were present when he told of the experience believed, his mannerism was such that we knew.

During the latter months of the war effort in France, Uncle Wayne and his platoon of six fellow soldiers were pinned down with small arms fire. There simply was no way to escape, the flash of the enemy's gun fire could be seen and heard just a short distance over there. The enemy was that close and moving directly toward the platoon, they knew they would be casualties in a matter of a few minutes.

A man in a uniform appeared, motioning for them to follow him. The man was dressed not only in military garb, but it was snow white. "Hurry and follow", Uncle Wayne did, along with the platoon members, the stranger didn't carry on a conversation, but in short order, led them to a bunker that was not too far away, one that would not be visible to the approaching enemy. Upon arriving safely, Uncle Wayne looked for the stranger to thank him for his help, the other platoon members were asking, "Who was that person and where did he come from, and where did he go?"

The platoon knew there were at lease eighteen enemies in the area. They could hear speaking but since their speech was in a foreign language, no one could understand what was being said. It was assumed the conversation was about the disappearance of their enemy. They waited several minutes after the sounds had faded before they left the hiding place.

There was only one way in and out of the small bunker that had been inserted in the side of small hill covered by bushes and the bushes were also covered with spider webs, Uncle Wayne was at the entrance, the stranger did not pass him going out, he simply was no longer present. None of the others could explain how the man disappeared, he simply was not present.

Each man searched their heart, individually, they knew, an Angel had led them to safety.

At times we asked to hear the story again, we heard it one time and one time only.

Acts 1:14–These all continued with one accord in Prayer …
What a Dream?

Norval had always considered himself to be a "man's man", that is if he thought about it at all, that's what he thought. Born in the late 1890s, in the red neck, blue-collar country in Kentucky.

An area well known for moon shine whisky, hard work and little if any respect for the law. The oldest of three children. The family was known as God

fearing Church going sort of people. But, times were tough and the young'n often didn't follow the leading and teaching of the parents. That kind of summed up the early years of Norval.

Left schooling after the eighth grade, which was about normal for boys in that time and area, there was lots of work to be done on the farm and not many hands to get the jobs done. Every hand was needed. Still he found time for his favorite recreation, just about the only recreation. Hunting squirrels was his favorite, he hunted by listening to noise in the trees and using a 22 rifle was all he needed, during the right time of the year, hunting rabbits was the thing to do. At least he brought some meat to the table. In early adulthood, he entered the trade as a Carpenter and became very skilled. His trade took him away from Kentucky; there were lots more jobs other places.

About the age of twenty-two, he married, soon there were other mouths to feed, but that was alright, times were prosperous and things were good. After all, it was the age of the flapper, with prohibition being the law of the land, the moon shine stills worked overtime, That was until late in the year of 1929, when the economy took a nose-dive with the onset of the "Great Depreciation".

It isn't easy not being able to provide for the family.

Not being able to provide, left only one way to face life, drink. Some people, some men are happy drunks, some are friendly drunks, others become mean. Norval was the later. As the years of the depreciation continued, drinking became worse. At some point, a neighbor invited the family to attend Church, all except Dad. Mother was raised in a family where everyone attended church each Sunday, Wednesday evening and during the semi-annual revival meetings. The family began to attend regularly, after a while; Norval attended with the family. Soon, he felt he was being called to be a minister, which was something with which he could not cope, he remaining silent about his feelings. The internal struggle continued several months, maybe years. The issue came to a conclusion following a dream. He wasn't sure it was a dream; in fact, he was convinced it was reality.

Later, he told and retold the dream, or vision, always wondering, was it a dream or was it real? During that night, the event played out, he found himself in Hell. Fire, burning brimstone was everywhere; those in attendance were screaming constantly, the Devil him self fought with the intent to prevent Norval from becoming a minister. The events were frightening. Upon waking, his face and body were covered with scratches, as were his bedclothes. His body reeked with the smell of smoke and burning sulfur,

There was no longer anything to decide it was his responsibility to become a minister of the Gospel. He was never able to determine if he experienced a dream or if he actually bodily descended into Hell. The reality was such although he couldn't be certain, he believed he physically experienced the event and it wasn't a dream.

Angels come in many forms

They were life long city dwellers, like many others, they had a small spot out in the country, a get a way place on a private lake. They visited the area a few times a year. Today was the first visit of the year; it had been a long, severe winter, they had not visited the area early this summer.

It was observed that mice had chewed the ducts throughout the cabin, it was not the first time it had happened, he determined it would be the last, the fiber ducts would be replaced with metal ones. The wife reached for the phone to call a carpenter friend to do the job. He would have none of that, he would do it. She tried to convince him he should not do it, but he insisted, "It was to be a messy and perhaps a dangerous project'" he didn't want anyone else to be exposed to the hazard.

The ducts had been installed in the craw space below the floor, without a basement, there was only a small crawl place of a couple of feet high, barely enough room to squeeze into, hardly enough to perform the task, safely was a concern. It required that one to lay on his back, working overhead in darkness with only a flashlight for guidance. He knew mice, rats, spiders of every description and other varmints could be present. The job needed to be done and he was determined he would be the one to do it.

Around noon, all of the needed equipment was procured and the task started. No sooner was the job started; a large white dog crawled under the house and laid beside the worker. Whenever he moved; the dog move likewise. Neither of them had ever seen the dog prior, they had no idea where it came from, there was no other house within a mile nor was there a name tag or other identification present. The job lasted four days; the dog was there the entire time, never leaving his side. The project was completed

away the tools, the dog disappeared. Both of them wondered, was the dog sent as an angel to keep watch during the job?

There is nothing that says an angel can not be in the body of a dog.

Max – Answered prayers

I f there was ever a dedicated Christian, Max was it. It seems he took after his grandpa; the story of Aquilla was his grandpa. Don't know much about his dad. His dad was Charlie. Charlie was born during the later years of the nineteenth century and was raised in the Kentucky area known then as the Land between the Rivers, today the area is known as the Land between the Lakes. As one would probably conclude, life was hard during his formative years, there was little in the way of employment. During the years of young adulthood, he managed to obtain a job working for the railroad in Wichita Kansas. Max grew up in Wichita Kansas.

God knows best, a*nd is still in the miracle business*

Recently while comparing stories, Max shared a time when only an answer to a prayer could and would resolve their situation; everyone knows that prayers are not answered these days. He related the following:

During a period when everything else failed, Max knew most of all he had failed, he believed he could take care of things by himself, he didn't need God, didn't want anything to do with God because of the manner in which Christians had acted and treated him. The desperate situation occurred as a result of major medical bill incurred as a result of a stroke suffered by his wife. It was obvious things could not become worse. Probably a major factor was his knowledge that the situation was in a large part the result of his own

19

Large rough hands covered his face in the darken kitchen weeping, filled with rage, a feeling of helplessness continued to engulf him. Knowing there was nothing he could do but ask a question for which he already had an answer, a question most of us ask from time to time. "Why, God, why has all of this happened to me, to us? Why?"

It was painfully easy to see and understand why, it certainly wasn't easy to admit it and come to grips with the reality. Some time before, he knowingly turned his back on the blessings of God and walked away. He vividly recalled the events and thinking, "If this is Christianity and these are Christians, I want nothing to do with it or them," he just walked away.

Over the years, many invited him to return to Church. Each time, the invitation was unwelcome and ignored, often not very pleasantly; he wanted nothing to do with those "Christians, anyone who could do those things." He was a Christian, not just a nominal one, but a faithful member of a local Church, but no more. They were unwelcome as was their friendship and believes. "Hypocrites". It made no difference, he wanted nothing to do with them and quickly let them know, in a not very friendly manner.

Mid November, he was sitting in the darkness because the electricity had been turned off, as was the telephone, water and heat. November meant that cold mid-west weather was here, it soon would get colder. The temperature outside was dropping, as was the temperature in the house. Cabinets were bare, the bank account empty. "Why? What do I do now?" "God, what can I do, I need help only you can deliver. I realize what I have done, you know why. I have nothing else to I can do and no where I can go." Memories of the past filled his numb mind.

Of course he realized the financial situation for the most part was generated because of the sickness of his wife. Some time prior, he had made a decision to give his wife all the love and support he could. He couldn't help thinking back about the time when he was driving a truck and it was routed through their hometown. He knew it was important for him to keep moving the truck since the load had to meet a dead line, but he stopped by home anyway. He found his wife lying on the floor, in very bad shape.

An ambulance was called to take Ann to the hospital. Doctors surely didn't give much hope that she would survive, much less improve so as to allow her to walk. The only thing that was important at that time was to give as much love and support as possible. He devoted his life to helping her. He realized his decision had brought them to this place. Regardless of the dire situation, there were no regrets, only concern of how they would get out of this mess. The only answer he could reach was prayer. For the first time in several years, he not only felt the need to pray, but he believed if anything was to help, it would have to be prayer. There was no reason to believe God would hear the pray of someone who deliberately walked away from the face of God and never looked back.

Edgar Allen Poe described the calling as a "rap, rap, rap." It wasn't that, more of a knock, knock, knock. Just sort of mild. He thought, I'm not expecting anyone and what ever it is can't be good. I'll ignore and they'll go away, there's no one I expect and there's no way that knock can be anything good. He remained with his face buried deep in the hands.

Shortly more knocking, this time, a little louder and more persistent, "I'll ignore it this time too." A few minutes later, more knocking, this time, much louder with authority. There was no reason to believe whoever it was was going to give up so he may as well see who it was. He peeked around the curtain observing two neatly dressed young men, neither of whom was recognized. The door was finally open, the men were greeted with, "whatever you're selling, you may as well go somewhere else, I just don't have money to buy anything even if I wanted to, and I don't want to."

"We're not selling anything," they verified the name and address, they were at the right place and looking for the right person. The purpose continued to be puzzling.

"Who are you, what do you want and why are you here?"

"We were asked to come and see you."

"The mystery continued, who asked you to come here and why?"

"The Church over a few blocks has collected some goods for you; we have it in the truck." Both of them went to the truck parked on the street in front of the house, returning in a few minutes, each with two large shopping bags of grocery bags, full and running over with foodstuff. The groceries were placed on the kitchen sink, they returned to the truck making four trips each. Each time returning with paper sacks brimming with food items along with other needed items, never had he seen such a mass of food.

At a time such as that, all that could be done was to sit and continue to cry, this time with joy. As they reached the door to leave, one reached into a pocket, bringing out an envelope. "The Church sent this to you also." They left, everything that had happened certainly seemed to be a dream, things like this just don't happen. An examination of the envelope revealed over four hundred dollars. Four hundred dollars and a kitchen full of groceries. He certainly couldn't grasp what had just happened.

For some time he continued in the dark, not knowing what do or what to say, he could only sit and weep with joy and thanksgiving. In what seemed to be only minutes, there was another knock at the front door. The first thought was, "They made a mistake and are coming back to get everything, that's cruel." A different set of men was standing there verifying they had the correct person and address. They were assured he was the one they were looking for. He continued in puzzlement, not knowing what was going on, they explained their purpose.

"We're from a Church, and pointed in the opposite direction of the two that had been with him just moments ago. We've been sent here to deliver some things to you." With that, they proceeded to make trip after trip to their truck, bringing in more than the first two. He continued in amazement.

"Things like this just don't happen, how can this be." There was no response; the sacks full of groceries just kept on coming until there was no place on the counter left to sit them. These two reached the front door to leave. Again just as the door closed, one reached into the coat pocket, removing a long white envelope and handed it. "Here, the Church also sent this." Both left him standing in amazement and shock.

This envelope contained over nine hundred dollars. More groceries than he had ever seen and over sixteen hundred dollars. In spite of everything, it was quickly determined that God is still in the business of answering prayers and is still in the miracle business. There was simply no other explanation for what had just happened. In spite of his recent attitude, God was still on His throne and in control.

Monday morning, the charges for electricity, telephone, water and heat were paid, they were soon restored, and he still had over six hundred dollars in his pocket.

His Way.

God is still on His throne and is in control.
    God doesn't work in coincidence.

Whenever we get involved in Christian endeavor, Satan gets busy. This was obvious as the Church's youth was returning Friday July 6th from the "Summer Youth Camp" held at Miracle Hills Ranch in Bethany, Missouri.

Some time after one PM Friday July 6th Satan really became active following a week during which the youth studied, played while worshipping and drawing closer to God. On their trip back home there were problems with the bus in which they were traveling. The Associate Pastor of the local Church contacted a Deacon advising him of the situation while asking for advice, the bus simply broke down on Interstate I-35, about 50 miles north of Kansas City. He was given some basic instructions, "check the level of the water and oil." he did, that was not the problem. The busload remained stranded.

From St. Louis it was tried via telephone to find help, first it was searched for a Ford dealer in the area, finding none but did locate a Ford rental agency near by and called them to see if they could be of assistance. The rental agency referred hum to an agency in Cameron Missouri, providing him their telephone number; the number was in turn provided to passed on. While all of this activity was under way, other Church members decided it was time to get

24

a pray chain in effect. it was explaining the situation. One of the members advised, "their son lives in Cameron."

While the prayer chain was in process, they continued to search via the Internet for a Baptist Church in the area where the bus was located, he located the "Bible Baptist Church" and called the church leaving a description of the situation.

It was explained her son attends the 1st Baptist Church in Cameron, and locates the phone number of the Church. The Church Secretary called and identified her self, he explained the emergency situation, the Church Secretary put the Church's Youth Pastor in action to help. That Church had a fifteen passenger van and brought the St. Louis group to the Cameron Church, getting them out of the heat.

The Deacon explained he had given the name of Midwest Auto and Diesel. The Church's Secretary advised they were members of that Church. Midwest Auto sent a man to check on the status of the bus, he determined the alternator was shot and needed to be replaced. The part had to be obtained from a supplier in Texas.

The youth were transported to the Church in Cameron and placed in the Church's Recreation room where they were provided Pizza and refreshments.

A group of Church members formed a caravan; several members drove to Cameron, gathered the youth and brought them back to the safety of the St. Louis Church building and their home.

The Church bus retrieved by a member as he returned from vacation.

This is the manner in which a Church is to act when there is problem, especially one affecting brother and Sister Christians, it is our responsibility to pray and act, in that order.

God will do His part.

The flood

For almost twenty years, she had served as a nurse for a few weeks each summer in Haiti. This summer was no exception so far; this year's service was not much different than other years. The old truck plowed through dusty roads as in the past. The area; in fact the entire Haiti half of the island was always hot and dry and dusty. This year it seemed to be dryer than usual. Driving the thirty something year old truck through the mountains' roads if they could be called roads, barely making it as a path. They always presented a challenge, if the motor didn't over heat, the breaks would fail, if that didn't happen, a tire would blow out, it was always something. The devils as always was alive and well in the mountains, especially in that part of the Country, in fact, the entire country. Today was no exception. Voodoo was the primary religion.

Everyone, all thirty-one of them were able to breathe a little easier; they were well acquainted with the area, feeling a little more comfortable now that the bottom of the mountain was in sight, the low lands as it was called. Temperature cooled a little, a little relief was received generated by the growing cloud cover up in the mountains where they had just left. It felt good, to be on the way home after two weeks. Each told themselves it was almost over; they would be down shortly. From somewhere in the distance, a strange noise was growing but they were unable to determine what it was or where it was coming from. What ever it was, it didn't sound good and it was getting louder and apparently closer.

A short distance up ahead, a dry riverbed lay waiting to be crossed. As rivers in that area went, it was bigger than most even dry it looked as a challenge. With steep banks and rock strewn bottom, it was always a challenge to cross, That unseen sound, whatever it was it grew louder and appeared to be closer, Well, not to worry, they were almost to the next stopping place and half way across the river bed.

A wall of water seemingly from no where surrounded the truck, water soon was gushing through the doors and becoming deeper by the second, they could feel the truck rise off its wheels, beginning to float, each looked at the others asking, "What can we do?" "What should we do?" Each looked at the others as one.

The answer, the only reasonable response, "We can pray." No time for the usual formalities, "Pray." The only prayer, "God save us!"

The old truck was a good five hundred feet from the other bank when the water hit, the truck was fast being washed down stream to destruction by the rushing water as the pray was offered. Immediately, the truck was on solid land on the other shore as the rushing rising water continued by.

No one asked how it happened, to a person, they knew, it was an answer to their prayer, an immediate answer.

Haiti-traffic court

H aiti, the very thought congers up thought of witchcraft and dark mysterious things. The thought could be right.

Haiti is situated about one hundred miles from Cuba between the Caribbean Sea and the North Atlantic Ocean; its approximately 17,250 square miles of land and 7,500,00 citizens shares the Western half of an island with the Dominican Republic. The island is about the only thing they share.

Haiti is one of the poorest lands in the Western hemisphere; its mostly very rough and mountainous, only about 20% of the land will support crops. 95% of the population is black or mixed race with the remaining 5% being white. Approximately one half of the population can read and write. The government is a Republic. 80% of the established religion is Roman Catholic and about 16% are protestant. Roughly one half of the population practices Voodoo. It is in this setting that a local missionary was led of the Holy Spirit to enter into mission work several years ago.

The leader had established two orphanages. He conducts mission trips several times a year, bringing needs, clothing and food items to those he could serve. The trips are hard and dangerous; he can only be successful by the power, guidance and leadership of the Holy Spirit.

The mode of transportation on the island is at best primitive. An old truck is the best transportation available. During one of the crusades with a group of College students, the Missionary was driving up the mountain road to turn around, the roads are too narrow to turn around anywhere except at the end of the trail. On this trip, a citizen tried to climb into the truck, during his attempt; the person fell and was slightly injured. The driver transported the injured person for medical treatment. The traffic laws inc the country are strict, very strict.

The fact the man was acting illegally did not matter, the Missionary was detained and taken to the local jail. Aware of the potential seriousness of the situation, he asked the Mission group to pray for his situation, knowing most anything could happen and he could be convicted of a traffic violation, his driving licenses taken away which would effectively end his ministry since he would have no means of transportation. Possibly more severe action could be handed out.

With the students earnestly praying, and the leader doing the only thing he could under the circumstances which was wait on the front porch of the police station, waiting and praying, two men approached him. Both Haitians were neatly and cleanly dressed and spoke English. The Missionary had been visiting in the area for several years and had never seen either one of them prior. They told him not to worry that everything was going to be OK. The three of them entered the station and was greeted by the police official. The two strangers took the police official off to one side and spoke with him quietly. After a few minutes, the Missionary was told to leave, that everything was OK. he never saw either of the strangers again.

Angels? He certainly thinks so!

Chilean miners

I'm sure you remember this story; it played before our eyes in the media daily toward the latter part of 2010.

When the miners came up one-at-a-time in that capsule–most were wearing special yellow Tshirts. These had been created by the Chilean branch of Campus Crusade for Christ. Emblazoned boldly across the front of the T-shirts were the words, in Spanish, "Thank you, Lord." The miners, in fact, had requested these words. The shirts were made and sent down to them while they waited for rescue.

But that's not all. A quotation on the back of the shirts which began "porque en su manostan..." was actually Scripture (Spanish). It was Psalm 95:4: "In His hands are the depths of the earth, the heights of the mountains are His also."

Campus Crusade had also provided the trapped miners–while still deep underground–with MP3 players with the audio version of the "Jesus" film. They also received the Bible in audio format.

Now here's the good news. Rev. Aldredo Cooper, the chaplain to the President of Chile, said of the rescued miners, "They're all wanting to testify to the Lord Jesus Christ. All 33 of them are saying that they found God in the mine. Five or six were already Christians and held services down in the mine. Many went down with no faith at all but they all say this: `We were not 33; we were 34 because Jesus Christ was with us down there."

One miner, Mario Sepulveda, told reporters, "We never lost faith. We knew we would be rescued. I have been with God and I've been with the devil. I seized the hand of God. I always knew God would get us out of there."

One interesting point that I had missed was that a medic actually was sent down the rescue hole before the other miners could be brought up. Isn't that a picture of what God did? He sent His Son down to us before we could be rescued. We all, like the miners, were in darkness. But, as Jesus said, "I am the light of the world. He who follows Me shall not walk in darkness, but have the light of life" (John 8:12). And, "I have come as a light into the world, that whoever believes in Me should not abide in darkness" (John 12:46).

I can only imagine the reaction, if those miners, trapped deep underground, came across Psalm 88 on their audio Bibles, when these words rang in their ears:I am counted with those who go down to the pit; I am like a man who has no strength, Adrift among the dead, Like the slain who lie in the grave, You have laid me in the lowest pit, In darkness, in the depths. You have put away my acquaintances far from me; I am shut up, and I cannot get out; My eye wastes away.. .LORD, I have called daily upon You; I have stretched out my hands to You. Will you work wonders for the dead?

(Psalm 88: 4-10, selected portions)

The Man Who Thanked the Sea gulls

Eddie Rickenbacker-Truth!

The story of a man who would routinely take a bucket of shrimp to the end of a pier and fed them to sea gulls. He would say "thank you" to them as he did. It turned out to be World War I military hero Eddie Rickenbacker who regarded a sea gull as the beginning of a series of events that saved his life while drifting for 24 days in a raft after a plane crash into the Pacific.

The story about the plane crash and the seagull is true and, as indicated in the Rumor, is an excerpt from a book by popular minister and inspirational author Max Lucado. The book is titled "In the Eye of the Storm."

Rickenbacker tells the story of the sea gulls in his autobiography. Rickenbacker was a pilot during WW I who became an ace and was presented with The Medal of Honor. The crash at sea took place in 1942 when he was sent by the U.S. government on a tour of the Pacific theater. The four-engine B-17 bomber on which he was a passenger went off course and ran out of fuel at sea.

Old Eddie. It happens every Friday evening, almost without fail, when the sun resembles a giant orange and is starting to dip into the blue ocean. Old Ed comes strolling along the beach to his favorite pier. Clutched in his bony hand is a bucket of shrimp. Ed walks out to the end of the pier, where it seems he almost has the world to himself. The glow of the sun is a golden bronze now. Everybody's gone, except for a few joggers on the beach. Standing out on the end of the pier, Ed is alone with his thoughts... .and his bucket of shrimp.

Before long, however, he is no longer alone. Up in the sky a thousand white dots come screeching and squawking, winging their way toward that lanky frame standing there on the end of the pier. Before long, dozens of seagulls have enveloped him, their wings fluttering and flapping wildly. Ed stands there tossing shrimp to the hungry birds. As he does, if you listen closely, you can hear him say with a smile, 'Thank you. Thank you.'

In a few short minutes the bucket is empty. But Ed doesn't leave. He stands there lost in thought, as though transported to another time and place. Invariably, one of the gulls lands on his sea-bleached, weather-beaten hat–an old military hat he's been wearing for years. When he finally turns around and begins to walk back toward the beach, a few of the birds hop along the pier with him until he gets to the stairs, and then they, too, fly away. And old Ed quietly makes his way down to the end of the beach and on home.

If you were sitting there on the pier with your fishing line in the water, Ed might seem like 'a funny old duck,' as my dad used to say. Or, 'a guy that's a sandwich shy of a picnic,' as my kids might say. To onlookers, he's just another old codger, lost in his own weird world, feeding the seagulls with a bucket full of shrimp.

To the onlooker, rituals can look either very strange or very empty. They can seem altogether unimportant... .maybe even a lot of nonsense. Old folks often do strange things, at least in the eyes of Boomers and Busters. Most of them would probably write Old Ed off, down there in Florida.

That's too bad. They'd do well to know him better. His full name: Eddie Rickenbacker. He was a famous hero back in World War II. On one of his flying missions across the Pacific, he and his seven-member crew went down. Miraculously, all of the men survived, crawled out of their plane, and climbed into a life raft. Captain Rickenbacker and his crew floated for days on the rough waters of the Pacific. They fought the sun. They fought sharks. Most of all, they fought hunger. By the eighth day their rations ran out. No food. No water. They were hundreds of miles from land and no one knew where they were. They needed a miracle.

That afternoon they had a simple devotional service and prayed for a miracle. They tried to nap. Eddie leaned back and pulled his military cap over his nose. Time dragged. All he could hear was the slap of the waves against the raft. Suddenly, Eddie felt something land on the top of his cap. It was a seagull! Old Ed would later describe how he sat perfectly still, planning his next move. With a flash of his hand and a squawk from the gull, he managed to grab it and wring its neck. He tore the feathers off, and he and his starving crew made a meal—a very slight meal for eight men—of it.

Then they used the intestines for bait. With it, they caught fish, which gave them food and more bait.. .and the cycle continued.

With that simple survival technique, they were able to endure the rigors of the sea until they were found and rescued. (after 24 days at sea...

Eddie Rickenbacker lived many years beyond that ordeal, but he never forgot the sacrifice of that first lifesaving seagull. And he never stopped saying, 'Thank you.' That's why almost every Friday night he would walk to the end of the pier with a bucket full of shrimp and a heart full of gratitude.

James 5:16—The affect fervent Prayer of a rightness man availath much

It is well with my Soul

The song "It Is Well With My Soul" was written by a successful Christian lawyer. He had two girls and a wife and the family planned a summer trip to go overseas.

Since he had a lot of work to do, he sent his family and decided to follow them later. He heard the news while on the following ship that another ship had capsized and he knew that his family was there since they mentioned the name of the ship.

On His return home, his Law firm was burned down and the insurance refused to pay, they said "It's An Act Of God". He had no money to pay for his house and no work, he also lost his house. Then while sitting and thinking what's happening to him, being a spiritual person, he wrote a song–whatever my Lord, you have taught me to say–It is well, it is well with my soul. My dear friend, a good attitude will determine your altitude.

When you look at your life, career, job or family life, what do you say? Do you praise God? Do you blame the devil? A good attitude towards God makes Him move on your behalf. Just sit down and say, Today God, it is well with my soul, I am thankful I had a peaceful sleep, I am thankful I am alive with possibilities, I am thankful have a roof over me, I am thankful I have a job, I am thankful that I have Family and Friends. Above all, I am thankful that I have the Lord Jesus Christ on my side.Be blessed and don't be envious or shocked when others are prospering because you don't know what they have been through to get there (test, trials and tribulation) so thank God for what you have. "Little is much when God is in it.

It Is Well With My Soul!

Touch someone's life with this message if God is for us, who can be against us?

God has seen you struggling with something.

God says it's over. A blessing is coming your way

Witnessing a miracle!

Two young police officers on routine patrol stopped an automobile for what is referred to as "reasonable cause". As is their assigned duty in that type situation, they directed the participants out of the car and to lean against the car so a routine search could be conducted,

In keeping with police procedures, while one of them "patted" one of the subjects, the second maintained surveillance from a few feet away from his partner and the subject being searched, also

The search was progressing routinely, until the pat down approached the belt area of the subject being searched when the subject pulled a revolver from his waist area, pointing the gun over his left shoulder and fired. The bullet struck the officer in the neck, severing a major artery. Immediately, blood was spurting everywhere, A second shot entered the officer's elbow. At that time the subject began to run, as he ran, another shot was fired striking the second officer in the leg.

The second officer was able to fire two shots at the fleeing subject as he ran, striking him with each shot. He continued about a block where he collapsed near the area where two of his buddies were standing. They assumed their friend had been the victim of a drive by shooting and flagged down a police car. The driver of the second police car was in the process of responding to an "officer down" call that had been made by the second officer. The subject was arrested without another incident, The officer in a second responding police car called for an ambulance for one of the officers, Because of the severity of the injury and the extreme *loss of* blood, the first officer was placed in the back seat of the police car for transportation to a hospital.

Following surgery, the attending doctor reported the surgery was successful, the officer was in critical condition, they would need to maintain a watchful eye on him for a few days, adding the officer who accompanied the injured man deserved and "should receive a commendation, without him, the officer would have never reached the hospital before he bled to death, he maintained pressure on the wound, stopping most of the bleeding."

The officer to whom the comment had been made was shocked and advised the doctor there was no one in the back seat with the wounded officer; the only one there was the injured man. The doctor continued to maintain there had to have been a second person applying pressure, there was no other explanation.

After a few moments of silence, the doctor finally realized he was being told the facts of the case, advised, "Gentlemen, you have just witnessed a miracle."

How would you explain the miracle?

Was the second person in the back seat an Angel?

Philiipns 4::6–Be careful for nothing, but in everything by Prayer and supplications with thanksgiving let you request be made known unto god

Another Room

No, not cold beneath the grasses,
Not close-walled within the tomb,
Rather, in our Father's mansion.
Living in another room.

Living, like the man who loves me,
Like my child with cheeks abloom,
Out of sight, at desk or schoolbook.
Busy, in another room.

Neither then by son whom fortune
Beckons where the strange lands loom,
Just behind the hanging curtain,
Serving in another room.

Shall I doubt my Father's mercy?
Shall I think of death as doom?
Or the stepping o'er the threshold
To a bigger, brighter room>

Shall I blame my Father's wisdom>
Shall I sit enswathed in gloom.

Sweet hour of prayer

When I know my loves are happy,
Waitinvg in another room?

author unknown

Moldova

T he first three questions regarding this country usually are: How do you pronounce it? How do you spell it? And, where is it? Let's take this one at a time. It is pronounced Mol-dol-va. The spelling is just the way the name sounds, the official name of the country is "Republic of Moldova." Where is it? All the way on the other side of the world.

If you were in school before 1991, you never studied about Moldova, it was not a country, until that year, it was a part of the Soviet Union.

Moldova is comprised of 32 counties, it is comprised of 13,000 square miles, about the size on the US State of Maryland, or a little more than 1/5 the size of Missouri. The population is about 4,400,000 compared with just over 5,600,000 in Missouri. The population in Moldova is the greatest of all the countries that were carved out of the old Soviet Union. In size, it is the second smallest country to come from the Soviet Union. It is the poorest of the countries that separated from the Soviet Union. The country is land locked, being bordered by Ukraine on the east and Romania on the west. The economy is primarily based on agriculture

The main religions: Christian Orthodox (93.3%), Baptist (1.0%) other religions include; Adventist, Roman Catholic and Jewish.

The literacy rate is high at 96%. Infant mortality is 11 for each 1,000 births. Life expectancy is 68.4 years.

This gives a view of the area into which Irene ventured on her missionary trip.

Irene

On the surface, Moldova seems an unlikely place to visit on a mission trip, especially the first mission trip ever under taken by someone. It was the first mission trip for Irene.

As it is written; God's ways are not our ways. He doesn't ask what we want to do or where we want to go, He knows what He wants us to do and where He wants us to go.

Mission trip to Moldova

The airplane to deliver the team left the St. Louis Airport July 14th, returning July 24th.

Irene's mission trip to Moldova began in the fellowship hall of Oak Hill Baptist Church December 14 during the Church's annual Mission Banquet. The speakers were Eric and Elaina Brewer, Missionaries to Moldova. The couple lives in this area and plan to move to Moldova later in September.

During that banquet, Irene felt that tug on her heart, that tug was to go to Moldova and help. The question of how the trip to Moldova would happen was not a determinate. A major element was, where will the expenses to finance the trip come from? Irene's decision was, that wasn't her concern, knowing that if it was God's will for her to go, God would provide.

God works in mysterious ways, and at the same time, expects us to do our part. Irene performed her part to raise funds, God did His part. The impossible happened; funds were raised permitting her to attend the missionary trip.

The citizens of the Country of Moldova have electricity, gas and telephone service; at least they do until Russia decides to turn it off. Russia may suspend service of the utilities at any time and seemingly for any reason and no reason. Most students had cell phones, so they were not without contact to the rest of the world. Team members were mildly surprised that the phones worked even in that area.

When the five team members in the mission trip arrived at the camp which would be their home during the period they would be in the area, they were received with a warm welcome. The American guests were provided a warm welcome.

The purpose of the mission camp was to teach Moldavians citizens English language. Some citizens had some knowledge of the language, to determine the level of t he training to be provided; each person was evaluated and placed in an appropriate section of the classes.

The primary religion in the Country is Orthodox. It is illegal to teach Christianity in the Communist country. As a means to over come this resistance, the Bible is used as a text book specifically, the book of Jeremiah. There was no interference with the teaching although the team was aware of the constant threat.

In many aspects, accommodations were primitive, because of those with whom the team made contact; the trip was a glorious experience.

Fourteen team members were assigned to each cabin and were responsible to maintain cleanliness. Showers were provided and available a short distance from the cabins. Without refrigeration, food and drink was neither hot nor cold, but was served at room temperature. Before the trip was concluded, they became accustomed to the food served in metal bowls, no plates; staple food consisted of cucumbers and bread.

Team members met wonderful people during the session. Heart wrenching stories of abuse of those involved in the studies were heard. Many of the stories had happy endings, many did not.

As the team said goodbye, the people being served expressed great thanks for the help they received from the team.

GOD'S "PHONE" NUMBER

Hello God, I called tonight
To talk a little while
I need a friend who'll listen
To my anxiety and trial.

You see, I can't quite make it
Through a day just on my own...
I need your love to guide me,
So I'll never feel alone.

I want to ask you please to keep,
My family safe and sound.
Come and fill their lives with confidence
For whatever fate they're bound.

Give me faith, dear God, to face
Each hour throughout the day,
And not to worry over things
I can't change in any way.

I thank you God, for being home
And listening to my call,
For giving me such good advice

When I stumble and fall!

Your number, God, is the only one
  That answers every time.
  I never get a busy signal,
  Never had to pay a dime.

So thank you, God, for listening
To my troubles and my sorrow.
Good night, God, I love You, too,
And I'll call again tomorrow!

THE FOLLOWING STORIES ARE FICTION. THEY ARE BASED ON INFORMATION WE ALREADY KNOW

Sometimes we let our imagine go wild. The following are examples. The stories are fiction, based upon what may and possibly could have happened.

Pump priming

In today's climate, when we hear the term "pump priming" our thoughts generally turn to economics with comments such as, "we need to put more money into the economy, we need to prime the pump to get business and the economy moving." Generally that is considered to be a good idea, at least it is considered to be so in some circles. That isn't what we're thinking about in this case, not today.

The story is told and often repeated, especially to individuals who spent a goodly amount of time in west Texas of a different kind of pump priming, an actual pump, the priming of which could be the difference between life and death.

Anyone who is knowledgeable about the span of Texas is aware that it seemingly goes on forever. Additionally especially in the summer, the heat is unbearable, about the only living thing one would see is an occasional jack rabbit, scorpion or armadillo with an occasional tumble weed blowing by, maybe a cloud drifting high overhead, but that isn't likely. A few miles south of Big Spring, just off the area where highways 33 and 158 intersect, over toward highways 87 and 163, in other words, kind of in the middle of nowhere there's an unlikely spot for a pump, or anything else.

It certainly isn't close to any of the highways, they're only mentioned to give one a general area for the location. One must wonder how it got there and why. Maybe at one time there was a road or path but if there once was, there isn't any longer. It's obvious from the condition, it's been there a long time. The note next to the pump relates to the condition. The writer of the note was well aware of human nature and as such, warns against succumbing to the idea of ignoring this message. The message printed and placed in a tin can and attached to the handle. There was no way to know how long the note had been there, it looked like it may have been there since there was first dirt anywhere. Just below the surface of the ground, there is a container with just the right amount of water to prime the pump if you don't drink any first. Look around, you'll see that if you yield to the temptation to drink before you prime the pump, there won't be enough to prime it. If you pour the water into the pump then pump, you'll have all of the fresh water you'll need. Be sure and leave some for the next person.

Sure enough there was a small container of water were the note said it would be. One in that situation would have a great temptation to drink the water, not trusting the pump. Norval looked around, seeing nothing for miles, he could see the premise of the note seemed to be relevant, the small amount of water wouldn't sustain him very long, so he may as well follow the instructions. With a sinking feeling, the water was poured into the pump, a gurgling sound was heard as the handle was pumped once, twice, three times. Down deep a sound was heard then water, plenty of water, cool water, enough to drink with plenty to fill empty canteens and plenty to refill the container as the note instructed.

It was not known who wrote the note, but whoever it was knew what they were doing. He left hopping the next person would also follow the words.

Ben, Just Checking In

This has been around before, still worth passing on... **God Bless**

The Minister, passing through his church In the middle of the day, Decided to pause by the altar To see who comes to pray.

Just then the back door opened, And a man came down the aisle, The minister frowned as he saw the man Hadn't shaved in a while.

His shirt was torn and shabby, And his coat was worn and frayed, The man knelt down and bowed his head, Then rose and walked away.

In the days that followed at precisely noon, The preacher saw this chap, Each time he knelt just for a moment, A lunch pail in his lap.

Well, the minister's suspicions grew, With robbery a main fear, He decided to stop and ask the man, 'What are you doing here?'

The old man said he was a factory worker And lunch was half an hour Lunchtime was his prayer time, For finding strength and power.

I stay only a moment Because the factory's far away; As 1 kneel here talking to the Lord, This is kinda what I say:

'I JUST CAME BY TO TELL YOU, LORD, HOW HAPPY I HAVE BEEN, SINCE WE FOUND EACH OTHERS FRIENDSHIP AND YOU TOOK AWAY MY SIN. DON'T KNOW MUCH OF HOW TO PRAY, BUT I THINK ABOUT YOU EVERY DAY. SO, JESUS, THIS IS BEN, JUST CHECKING IN TODAY.'

The minister feeling foolish, Told Ben that it was fine. He told the man that he was welcome To pray there anytime.

'It's time to go, and thanks,' Ben said As he hurried to the door. Then the minister knelt there at the altar, Which he'd never done before. His cold heart melted, warmed with love, As he met with Jesus there. As the tears flowed down his cheeks, He repeated old Ben's prayer:

'I JUST CAME BY TO TELL YOU, LORD, HOW HAPPY I'VE BEEN, SINCE WE FOUND EACH OTHERS FRIENDSHIP AND YOU TOOK AWAY MY SIN. I DON'T KNOW MUCH OF HOW TO PRAY, BUT I THINK ABOUT YOU EVERYDAY. SO, JESUS, THIS IS ME, JUST, CHECKING IN TODAY.'

Past noon one day, the minister noticed That old Ben hadn't come. As more days passed and still no Ben, He began to worry some. At the factory, he asked about him, Learning he was ill. The hospital stall was worried, But he'd given them a thrill.

The week that Ben was with them, Brought changes in the ward. His smiles and joy contagious. Changed people were his reward. The head nurse couldn't understand Why Ben could be so glad, When no flowers, calls or cards came, Not a visitor he had.

The minister stayed by his bed, He voiced the nurse's concern: No friends had come to show they cared. he had no where to turn. Looking surprised, old Ben spoke up And with a winsome smile; 'The nurse is wrong, she couldn't know, He's been here all the while.'

Everyday at noon He comes here, A dear friend of mine, you see, He sits right down and takes my hand, Leans over and says to me:

'I JUST CAME BY TO TELL YOU, BEN, HOW HAPPY I HAVE BEEN, SINCE WE FOUND THIS FRIENDSHIP, AND I TOOK AWAY YOUR SIN. I THINK ABOUT YOU ALWAYS AND I LOVE TO HEAR YOU PRAY, AND SO BEN, THIS IS JESUS, JUST CHECKING IN TODAY.'

If this blesses you, pass it on. Many people will walk in and out of your life, but only true friends will leave footprints in your heart May God hold you in the palm of His hand And Angels watch over you.

Jesus said. 'If you are ashamed of me. I will be ashamed Of you before my Father.'

Romans 8:26–... *But the Spirit itself maketh intercession for us with groaning, which cannot be uttered*

A Visit from a friend

had a visit from a friend this morning.

He arrived early, sat down with me and chatted with me for a while about how things were currently going for me in my life.

After carefully and compassionately listening to all that I had to say, He stood up, walked over to me, leaned over and gently held me for a while.

Then, after reassuring me not to worry, that everything would work out for me and be just fine, He asked me if I knew of anyone else that could use a visit from Him.

I immediately thought of you, my friend.

I gave Him your name, and He knew where you lived. He gave me another reassuring hug, thanked me and I walked with Him to my front door. He told me that He was on His way to your place.

When He gets to your place, escort Him to the next stop. Please don't forget others who need Him. The message He is carrying is very important.

I asked Him to bless you and yours with peace, happiness and abundance.

Say a prayer and then guide Him on to bless others as I sent him on to bless you. Our assignment is to spread love, respect and kindness throughout the world.

Have a blessed day and touch somebody's life today as hopefully I have touched your life. He's walking around the world!

Wherever and whenever He is invited.

Four Boyfriends

Once upon a time there was this girl who had four boyfriends.

She loved the 4th boyfriend the most and adorned him with rich robes and treated him to the finest of delicacies. She gave him nothing but the best.

She also loved the 3rd boyfriend very much and was always showing him off to neighboring kingdoms. However, she feared that one day he would leave her for another.

She also loved her 2nd boyfriend. He was her confidant and was always kind, considerate and patient with her. Whenever this girl faced a problem, she could confide in him, and he would help her get through the difficult times.

The girl's st boyfriend was a very loyal partner and had made great contributions in maintaining her wealth and kingdom. However, she did not love the first boyfriend. Although he loved her deeply, she hardly took notice of him!

One day, the girl fell ill and she knew her time was short. She thought of her luxurious life and wondered, I now have four boyfriends with me, but when I die, I'll be all alone.'

Thus, she asked the 4th boyfriend, 'I loved you the most, endowed you with the finest clothing and showered great care over you. Now that I'm dying, will you follow me and keep me company?' 'No way!' replied the 4th boyfriend, and he walked away without another word.

His answer cut like a sharp knife right into her heart.

The sad girl then asked the 3rd boyfriend, 'I loved you all my life. Now that I'm dying, will you follow me and keep me company?'

'No!', replied the 3rd boyfriend. 'Life is too good! When you die, I'm going to marry someone else!'

Her heart sank and turned cold.

She then asked the 2nd boyfriend, 'I have always turned to you for help and you've always been there for me. When I die, will you follow me and keep me company?'

'I'm sorry, I can't help you out this time!', replied the 2nd boyfriend. 'At the very most, I can only walk with you to your grave.' His answer struck her like a bolt of lightning, and the girl was devastated.

Then a voice called out: 'I'll go with you. I'll follow you no matter where you go.'

The girl looked up, and there was her first boyfriend. He was very skinny as he suffered from malnutrition and neglect.

Greatly grieved, the girl said, 'I should have taken much better care of you when I had the chance!'

In truth, you have 4 boyfriends in your lives:

Your 4th boyfriend is your body. No matter how much time and effort you lavish in making it look good, it will leave you when you die.

Your 3rd boyfriend is your possessions, status and wealth. When you die, it will all go to others.

Your 2nd boyfriend is your family and friends. No matter how much they have been there for you, the furthest they can stay by you is up to the grave.

And your 1st boyfriend is your Soul. Often neglected in pursuit of wealth, power and pleasures of the world.

However, your Soul is the only thing that will follow you where ever you go. Cultivate, strengthen and cherish it now, for it is the only part of you that will follow you to the throne of God and continue with you throughout Eternity. Thought for the day: Remember, when the world pushes you to your knees, you're in the perfect position to pray.

The Attorney

After living what I felt was a "decent" life, my time on earth came to the end. The first thing I remember is sitting on a bench in the waiting room of what I thought to be a courthouse. The doors opened and I was instructed to come in and have a seat by the defense table.

The corner door flew open and there appeared the Judge in full flowing robes. He commanded an awesome presence as He moved across the room. I couldn't take my eyes off of Him. As He took His seat behind the bench, He said, "Let us begin."

The prosecutor rose and said, "My name is Satan and I am here to show you why this man belongs in hell." He proceeded to tell of lies I told, thngs I stole, and in the past when I cheated others. Satan told of other horrible perversions once in my life and the more he spoke, the further down in my seat I sank I was so embarrassed, I couldn't look at anyone, even my own Attorney, as the Devil told of sins even I completely forgotten about. As upset as I was at Satan for telling all these things about me, I was equally upset at My Attorney who sat there silently not offering any form of defense at all. I know I was guilty of those things, but I did some good in my life—couldn't that at least equal out part of the harm I'd done?

Satan finished with a fury and said, "This man belongs in hell, he is guilty of all I have charged and there is not a person who can prove otherwise."

When it was His turn, My Attorney first asked if He might approach the bench The Judge allowed this over the strong objection of Satan, and beckoned Him to come forward. As He got up and started walking, I was able to see Him in His full splendor and majesty. I realized why He seemed so familiar; this was Jesus representing me, my Lord and my Savior.

He stopped at the bench and softly said to the Judge, "Hi, Dad," then He turned to address the court. "Satan was correct in saying this man sinned, I won't deny any of these allegations. And, yes, the wage of sin is death, and this man deserves to be punished."

Jesus took a deep breath and turned to His Father with outstretched arms and proclaimed, "However, I died on the cross so this person might have eternal life and he accepted Me as his Savior, so he is Mine."

My Lord continued with, "His name is written in the Book of Life and no one can snatch him from Me. Satan still does not understand yet. This man is not to be given justice, but rather mercy."

As Jesus sat down, He quietly paused, looked at His Father and said, "There is nothing else that needs to be done. I've done it all."

The Judge lifted His mighty hand and slammed the gavel down. The following words bellowed from His lips... "This man is free. The penalty for him was already paid in full. Case dismissed"

As my Lord led me away, I could hear Satan ranting and raving, "I won't give up, I will win the next one."

I asked Jesus as He gave me my instructions where to go next, "Have you ever lost a case?" Christ lovingly smiled and said, "Everyone that comes to Me and asked Me to represent them, received the same verdict as you,

"PAID IN FULL."

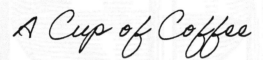

A Cup of Coffee

A group of alumni, highly established in their careers, got together to visit their old university professor. Conversation soon turned into complaints about stress in work and life.

Offering his guests coffee, the professor went to the kitchen and returned with a large pot of coffee and an assortment of cups porcelain, plastic, glass, crystal, some plain looking, some expensive, some exquisite—telling them to help themselves to the coffee.

When all the students had a cup of coffee in hand, the professor said: 'If you noticed, all the nice looking expensive cups were taken up, leaving behind the plain and cheap ones.

While it is normal for you to want only the best for yourselves, that is the source of your problems and stress. Be assured that the cup itself adds no quality to the coffee. In most cases it is just more expensive and in some cases even hides what we drink. What all of you really wanted was coffee, not the cup, but you consciously went for the best cups ... And then you began eyeing each other's cups.

Now consider this: Life is the coffee; the jobs, money and position in society are the cups. They are just tools to hold and contain Life, and the type of cup we have does not define, nor change the quality of Life we live. Sometimes, by concentrating only on the cup, we fail to enjoy the coffee God has provided us." God brews the coffee, not the cups .... Enjoy your coffee!

"The happiest people don't have the best of everything. They just make the best of everything."

Live simply. Love generously. Care deeply. Speak kindly. Leave the rest to God.

The Big Wheel

I n September 1960, I woke up one morning with six hungry
babies and just 75 cents in my pocket. Their father was gone.
The boys ranged from three months to seven years; their sister was
two. Their Dad had never been much more than a presence they
feared. Whenever they heard his voice, they hid in their beds. He
did manage to leave $15 a week to buy groceries. Now that he had
decided to leave, there would be no more beatings, but no food
either. If there was a welfare system in effect in southern Indiana
at that time, I certainly knew nothing about it. I scrubbed the kids.

The seven of us went to every factory, store and restaurant in
our Small town. No luck. The kids stayed crammed into the car and
tried to be quiet while I tried to convince whomever would listen
that I was willing to learn or do anything. I had to have a job. Still
no luck. The last place we went to, just a few miles out of town,
was an old Root Beer Barrel drive-in that had been converted to a
truck stop. It was called the Big Wheel.

An old lady called Granny owned the place and she peeked
out of the window from time to time at all those kids. She needed
someone on the graveyard shift, eleven at night until seven in the
morning. She paid .65 cents an hour and I could start that night. I
raced home and called the teenager down the street that baby-sat
for people.

I bargained with her to come and sleep on my sofa for a dollar
a night. She could arrive with her pajamas on and the kids would

already be asleep. This seemed like a good arrangement to her, so we made a deal. That night when the little ones and I knelt to say our prayers, we all thanked God for finding Mommy a job. And so I started at the Big Wheel .medical needs, clothing and food items to those he can serve. The trips are hard and dangerous; he can only be successful by the power, guidance and leadership of the Holy Spirit.

When I got home in the mornings I woke up the baby-sitter and sent her home with one dollar of my tip money, fully half of what I averaged every night. As the weeks went by, heating bills added a strain to my meager wage. The tires on the old Chevy had the consistency of penny balloons and began to leak. I had to fill them with air on the way to work and again every morning before I could go home. One bleak fall morning, I dragged myself to the car to go home and found four tires in the back seat. New tires! There was no note, no nothing, just those beautiful brand new tires. Had angels taken up residence in Indiana? I wondered.

I made a deal with the local service station. In exchange for his mounting the new tires, I would clean up his office. I remember it took me a lot longer to scrub his floor than it did for him to do the tires. I was now working six nights instead of five and it still wasn't enough. Christmas was coming and I knew there would be no money for toys for the kids. I found a can of red paint and started repairing and painting some old toys. Then hid them in the basement so there would be something for Santa to deliver on Christmas morning. Clothes were a worry too. I was sewing patches on top of patches on the boy's pants and soon they would be too far gone to repair.

On Christmas Eve the usual customers were drinking coffee in the Big Wheel. These were the truckers, Less, Frank, and Jim, and a state Trooper named Joe. A few musicians were hanging around after a gig at the Legion and were dropping nickels in the pinball machine. The regulars all just sat around and talked through the wee hours of the morning and then left to get home before the sun came up.

When it was time for me to go home at seven o'clock on Christmas Morning I hurried to the car. I was hoping the kids wouldn't wake up before I managed to get home and get the presents from the basement and place them under the tree. (We had cut down a small cedar tree by the side of the road down by the dump.) It was still dark and I couldn't see much, but there appeared to be some dark shadows in the car...or was that just a trick of the night? Something certainly looked different, but it was hard to tell what.

When I reached the car I peered warily into one of the side windows. Then my jaw dropped in amazement. My old battered Chevy was filled to the top with boxes of all shapes and sizes. I quickly opened the driver's side door, crumbled inside and kneeled in the front facing the back seat.

Reaching back, I pulled off the lid of the top box. Inside was whole case of little blue jeans, sizes 2-10. I looked inside another box: It was full of shirts to go with the jeans. Then I peeked inside some of the other boxes. There was candy and nuts and bananas and bags of groceries. There was an enormous ham for baking, and canned vegetables and potatoes. There was pudding and Jell-O and cookies, pie filling and flour.

There was whole bag of laundry supplies and cleaning items. And there were five toy trucks and one beautiful little doll. As I drove back through empty streets as the sun slowly rose on the most amazing Christmas Day of my life, I was sobbing with gratitude. And I will never forget the joy on the faces of my little ones that precious morning.

Yes, there were angels in Indiana that long-ago December. And they all hung out at the Big Wheel truck stop....THE POWER OF PRAYER. God still sits on the throne; the devil is a liar. You may be going through a tough time right now but God is getting ready to bless you in a way that only He can. Keep the faith! Prayer is powerful, and prayer is one of the best gifts we receive. There is no cost but a lot of rewards.

Let's continue to pray for one another.

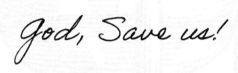

God, Save us!

This may not be factual, but, it could have been. We won't know until that day!

I t was 1993, that summer, a massive flood covered much of the Midwest. The Mississippi River and the Missouri river and the Illinois rives melted into what could have been described as the Mid-America Lake. The flood continued for about six months

Many were forced from their homes as the water expanded. For reasons know only to themselves, some stayed in their house. Silas and his family did not leave; they prayed that God would deliver them. A very realistic thing to do. "God save us."

They continued to pray as the water reached the foundation, a Police officer making rounds warning everyone to leave the area because the high water forecast. Silas stated, "We don't need to leave, God will provide."

The water reached the second floor, the family had now moved to that level. A motor boat came by, the operator encouraged the family to leave while there was still time. Silas said, "We will stay, God will provide."

Awhile later, the family had moved to the roof, the water splashed the eaves. A last ditch effort to save the few remaining residence, a helicopter flew by; the pilot encouraged the family to get on board and fly to safety. As his wont, Silas responded, "God will provide."

Soon, the family awoke in Heaven, Silas addressed God, "I trusted you, I prayed for rescue and here we are, why did you not hear and answer my prayers?"

Softly, God replied, "I sent a Police officer to help followed by someone in a boat followed by a helicopter, what more did you want?"

God's answer isn't always what we want and expect.

Unanswered prayers

There is a story similar to the one entitled "What happens in Heaven when we pray." The story goes like this. We can't promise it to be true, although, the concept is.

Mr. Smith a long time Deacon in the local Baptist Church died and immediately was warmly received at the Pearly Gates by St. Peter. Greetings by his friends who had preceded him kept him busy for a while as he renewed old acquaints. All of his life, he had heard of the splendor of Heaven and he was anxious to see it for himself and asked for a tour. After a time, they came to a building the looked just like a warehouse his Company used on earth to store various items.

Wanting to absorb all he could, he proceeded to ask the guide, "What is that?"

"The casual reply, "just storage of unused items."

"What kind of items? I had no idea Heaven had unused items. Can we look in there so I can better understand the type of unused items stored in Heaven?"

St. Peter advised against the idea and continued to walk.

Mr. Smith just couldn't let it go and continued to badger St. Peter. "I really want to know everything, what type of items could possibly be stored in Heaven. Not only that, but the building was huge. What could possibly be stored that needs a building that big. St. Peter continued to walk advising Mr. Smith knowing which items stored in the building would not be in his, (Mr. Smith') best interest. They continued to walk

Mr. Smith had been an executive while on earth and was not used to being told no, He continued to ask not only what was in the building, but he wanted to go in and see. Finally, even the patience's of St. Peter was tried, after a while, he agreed to open the door and go in. He did so with a warning that it was not a good idea. They entered anyway.

The items were neatly stacked in boxes. The boxes were stacked as high as he could see in rows that seemed to stretch for ever. Mr. Smith was as interested as ever, perhaps more so. The next question was, "I noticed names on each box, is there a box with my name on it?"

"Yes." St. Peter moved on.

It was obvious the boxes were stored in alphabetic order. There was no waiting; he was running to find his box. It wasn't in the last row, but was close enough since his name was toward the end of the alphabet. It was sealed; of course Mr. Smith wanted it opened. St. Peter advised against it, advising no one who has ever opened one of the boxes was ever happy. That explanation did not pacify. Has was his usual custom, there was continued begging until St. Peter gave in and opened the box.

The box was full to the point of running over, all sorts of things. Mr. Smith almost to the point of being angry, announced, "Everything in there is something I wanted while on earth but was never able to obtain."

"Yes, we know, everything in that box, in fact, everything in this building are items, waiting to be given to individuals on earth, but they were not, simply because the possible recipients never asked God for them. I'm sure you remember, you were told, that God knows what you have need of and is just waiting for you to ask. You never asked, therefore, the things stayed here in Heaven."

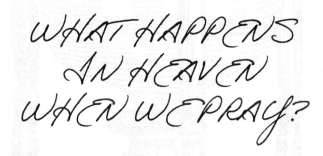

WHAT HAPPENS IN HEAVEN WHEN WE PRAY?

"**S**o sad," the angel sighed. "After people receive the blessings that they asked for, very few send back acknowledgments."

"How does one acknowledge God's blessings?" I asked.

"Simple," the angel answered. Just say, "Thank you, Lord."

"What blessings should they acknowledge?" I asked.

"If you have food in the refrigerator, clothes on your back, a roof overhead and a place to sleep you are richer than 75% of this world.

If you have money in the bank, in your wallet, and spare change in a dish, you are among the top 8% of the world's wealthy, and if you get this on your own computer, you are part of the 1% in the world who has that opportunity."

"If you woke up this morning with more health than illness.. You are more blessed than the many who will not even survive this day."

"If you have never experienced the fear in battle, the loneliness of imprisonment, the agony of torture, or the pangs of starvation... You are ahead of 700 million people in the world."

"If you can attend a church without the fear of harassment, arrest, torture or death you are envied by, and more blessed than, three billion people in the world."

"If your parents are still alive and still married.... you are very rare."

"If you can hold your head up and smile, you are not the norm, you're unique to all those in doubt and despair..."

"Ok," I said. "What now? How can I start?"

The Angel said, "If you can read this message, you just received a double blessing in that someone was thinking of you as very special and you are more blessed than over two billion people in the world who cannot read at all."

Have a good day, count your blessings, and if you care to, pass this along to remind everyone else how blessed we all are...

Philippians 4:6 ... with Thanksgivings let your request be known unto God

Victory, God's way

This writing is fiction; it should be and must be recognized as such. During this epistle, the happenings are based in the Biblical recording of the book of Joshua and the vivid imagination of the writer.

It is important to remember that people are basically the same today as they were over 3,000 years ago in 1,450 BC. There were no newspapers, television, radio or even the cell phone for communication and the sharing and delivering of information. The mode was simply via oral communication.

The following is fictionalized dialogue of ordinary citizens, we know people had conversations regarding the events of the day and times were conducted the same as with individuals of our time,

1st Thessalonians 5:17–Pray without ceasing

Across the river

S tanding on the pathway with the massive stone walls protecting the large ancient city which stood just a short distance from the river they had crossed just a few days before. The line of people seemed to stretch for ever. The rising sun was starting to peek over the Eastern tree lined skyline.

Though the throng was large, sounds remained subdued. Speaking in hushed quiet tones, Abbie commentated to his friend Jacob, "do you understand what we are doing and why? Our commander advised us that Joshua has said that we are to fight a battle and that God has told him we will be successful. So far all we have done is walk around this city, there hasn't been any fighting. I don't understand how our small army will be successful against this city."

"This sure is a strange battle, not at all like the ones we fought while we were on the other side of the river in the wilderness, the Midannites. Jakaz, Basham and others."

"We've marched around this city wall for six days; our leader has said that today we'll go seven times around. I was tired going around one time; I'm not sure how I'll do after seven times. None of this makes any sense. I just wish we would do something besides walk. We've been told this is Joshua's instruction, he has been right in the past, I'm sure he is now."

Jacob seem to be of the same opinion as his friend, he excitedly called out, "I see the Priests and the Ark way up there, they're starting to move, now, we'll see something happen." The line of people started to move, it stretch forever, at least that's the way it looked.

The line walked in subdued quietness, they had no idea what to expect and they were ready for anything that could happen, anything could occur at any time. My whole life has been that of the military, "remember the battles we fought when we defeated the armies at Jahaz and Basham, we were out numbered but we won anyway. Josuha was the leader of our army, of course, that was before Moses died, there shouldn't be any difference now that he has replaced Moses."

Jacob continued, almost as if talking to himself, "what did you think about the river we crossed a few days ago? I remember the stories my father described of the events as this throng left Egypt and how Moses led them to the Red Sea, I also remember him telling us about the cloud we followed by day and a pillar of fire at night, we, ended up at the Red Sea, the problem father said was the sea was at flood stage, there was no way to cross, he said everyone was upset with Moses since it looked as if they were going to be trapped. In the distance they could see dust raised by the Egyptian army that was chasing them. Just when everything appeared to be lost, the water parted, piled up and the next day everyone walked across on dry land. He also said that when everyone was across; the Egyptian army started to follow the same path, when they got to the middle of the sea, the water rushed back and drown all of the Egyptian army . He said that got everyone's attention.

"One of the first things they did after crossing the sea was to build an alter and give thanks to God for their deliverance. Kind of like us crossing the river a few days ago. God had to be in control. Let's hope He will be in control of this so called battle."

I'm older than you, you were born while we were in the wilderness, I was about six years old at the time we left Egypt, too young to understand what was going on, I do remember the crossing, I remember sticking my hand into the bank of water, of course, my hand got wet and my mother fussed at me to stop it. The other boys were doing the same. But, that was a long time ago."

"During the trip from Egypt, my mother and father have died. My mother's brother died in one of the many battles fought along the way. I thought this battle would be just like the others, it sure hasn't been the same so far, there hasn't been any battle at all. I'm not sure our small army can stand against the larger army that's on the other side of this wall. Have you noticed the number of soldiers on top of the wall and how they watch us as we march around?"

Abbie had been silent as Jacob talked; he thought Jacob was talking so much because he was nervous and afraid, he may have been correct. The day was getting late as they marched as they ended the seventh trip."

In the distance, the sound of trumpets was heard; as was shouting, the sound was mixed with the loud noise created by the collapse of the surrounding wall, the entire wall fell, it dropped straight down, all of the wall all of the way around the city. Shouts could be heard mixed with noise of people running. Israelites would like to have poured into the city to live, but Joshua had said that God had stated the city of Jericho would never have residences again. The inhabitants of Jericho were surprised. Every citizen of Jericho fled, including the army. Joshua had given word that he had received from God that no one not even animals were to be saved alive. In short manner, God's word had been followed.

Joshua's instructions included that no one was to take anything as booty, not even an animal. Everything and everyone was to be destroyed. The gold, silver, iron and brass items were to become a part of the treasury of God.

Jacob thought, Israelite families would like to have immediately begun to settle in the now deserted city, but the city had been destroyed and burned, that was not an option.

On to Ai

*R**emember, the following is a fictional account of the events cited in the bible – Joshua chapters 7 & 8***

The Israelites were getting settling in their new abode, it was much like the home they had during the past years. A short distance from the River Jordan, but that was all that was different. It had been a long time since they had a place to call home. This was not what they wanted for their new home land. Joshua reminded them that God had given them the land, but they had to claim it.

"Abbie, what do you think about the latest story that Joshua sent a few men to view out the city of Ai so plans can be made as we move out to take more of the area, Joshua continues to remind that it's God's plan for us to take the entire area. The report of the spies was the military of Ai was neither strong nor great in number. Their recommendation was to send only a limited number of soldiers since Ai's defenses were meager.

A few days later, Joshua followed the suggestions of the spies, he sent only about three thousand soldiers to attack Ai. It was soon reported to Joshua of the results of their actions, he was distressed with the results and the report.

There was no doubt in the mind of Joshua's that God had instructed him to capture all the land from the Great sea to the Euphrates River and now the army had been defeated, His Question of God was why? A smaller army had defeated the Israel army. Still the question, why? They were a long way off from capturing the area God had given them.

Abbie, thinking out loud, if I had been in the number that attacked Ai, there would have been a different outcome. Joshua continued to ask God why? The reply was that someone in the camp had disobeyed God's command that nothing was to be taken except the items which were to go into the treasury of God. Someone had disobeyed God's command. It was Joshua's responsibility to determine who and why.

Jacob commented. "I heard that Joshua commanded people from every tribe to report to him until the person who was guilty was discovered. It took a while, but the person who was guilty was found."

Abbie responded, "I heard Joshua found the items that had been taken in the tent of the person who took them. The person had to know taking them was wrong or he would not have hidden the items under the floor of his tent. I understand Joshua had the person and his family executed. Again this action was God's direction."

Jacob commented, "The next time Ai, was attacked. A greater number of soldiers were sent. The outcome was much different, this time, God's plan was followed.

As always, doing things God's way works out best.

Romans 12:12–…. Continue in Prayer

Visitors from a far country

F or addition to this story, visit the Bible, Matthew chapter 2 and Luje chapter 2

What is causing all of the noise out in front? There's a large gathering of all sorts of people out there; some are dressed very nicely, especially for this area.

Mary and Joseph gathered around the door, searching to determine what all the fuss meant, a large gathering had stopped in the street in from of the house, several camels and their riders appeared to be searching for something, the leader of the group was conversing with other members. Now they're coming to the door, what's going on? They're dressed fancy, they're carrying some small packages, the packages were gifts for the baby.

The group appeared to be someone of importance. "What are they doing in this neighborhood?"

The house wasn't large enough to accommodate the large group; some milled around out side the house, while the animals quietly knelt.

"We have seen the star and followed as it led us for a long time, we know the Prophets said something like this would happen. We came to pay homage to the King. We stopped and asked directions from King Herod, he asked us to stop again on our way back home, he said he wanted to also pay respect. However, we were visited by an angel who advised us to go home by a different route and we will."

These events brought back memories from a couple of year's prior when she and Joseph had to go from Nazareth to Bethlehem because Caesar Augustus mandated that everyone must go their city of birth for a census. The trip was very long, requiring a couple of days to make the trip, When we arrived we couldn't find a place to stay so we had to stay in a stable with the animals, not only that, I gave birth to our baby boy who is now two years old.

There were several animals housed in the stable along with others who also couldn't find a room. One of the touching events was when a few shepherds came into the stable. They said they witnessed a wonderful event, the sky filled with angels singing praises to God, we had to come into the town to see what was going on.

I was thankful that there was a large group of others going along on the trip, it gave us protection, there are always crimes along that route. Thankfully, we didn't experience any.

The visitors didn't stay long, and soon after they left, Joseph received a visit from an angel who advised that we should immediately go to Egypt for safety since King Herod had put out a decree that all boys age two years old and younger were to be killed. It was a few years before Joseph received another visit telling us it was OK to return, King Herod was dead.

John 15:17 "If you abide in Me and My word abides in you, you will ask whatever you desire and it shall be done unto you."

First day of the week

For additional information, visit the Bible, Matthew chapter 2

Hold the torch out in front, I can't see where I'm going, we want to be there before it gets light, there's no telling what we'll encounter when we get there.

Daylight was breaking as they arrived, the torch gave some light, the three collectively wondered, "how will we get in, that large boulder is blocking the entrance, it's too lager for any of us to move it. We must get inside; we have the perfume to give the body the necessary preparation for burial, we didn't have time on Friday."

Drawing near to the area, something just didn't seem right, the soldiers assigned to guard the tomb were not in place, the stone closing the opening was already moved, maybe the earthquake experience this morning had moved it, at least it was moved. Nothing seems to be as we expected.

The three ran into the opening, the body was not there, the grave clothing were neatly resting near where they had expected the body to rest. Fear and confusion filled the air. A voice from a man dressed in shinning white garments seated nearby that they hadn't noticed gently spoke, "He's not here, He has risen as He said." They determined him to be an Angel.

The Angel urged then to "go and tell Peter and the others what they had seen.

1st Thessalonians 5:17 "Pray without ceasing"

A Father, a Daughter and a Dog

"**W**atch out! You nearly broad sided that car!" My father yelled at me. "Can't you do anything right?"

Those words hurt worse than blows. I turned my head toward the elderly man in the seat beside me, daring me to challenge him. A lump rose in my throat as I averted my eyes. I wasn't prepared for another battle.

"I saw the car, Dad. Please don't yell at me when I'm driving."

My voice was measured and steady, sounding far calmer than I really felt.Dad glared at me, then turned away and settled back. At home I left Dad in front of the television and went outside to collect my thoughts.... Dark, heavy clouds hung in the air with a promise of rain. The rumble of distant thunder seemed to echo my inner turmoil. What could I do about him?

Dad had been a lumberjack in Washington and Oregon. He had enjoyed being outdoors and had reveled in pitting his strength against the forces of nature. He had entered grueling lumberjack competitions, and had placed often. The shelves in his house were filled with trophies that attested to his prowess.

The years marched on relentlessly. The first time he couldn't lift a heavy log, he joked about it; but later that same day I saw him outside alone, straining to lift it. He became irritable whenever anyone teased him about his advancing age, or when he couldn't do something he had done as a younger man.

Four days after his sixty-seventh birthday, he had a heart attack. An ambulance sped him to the hospital while a paramedic administered CPR to keep blood and oxygen flowing.

At the hospital, Dad was rushed into an operating room. He was lucky; he survived. But something inside Dad died. His zest for life was gone. He obstinately refused to follow doctor's orders. Suggestions and offers of help were turned aside with sarcasm and insults. The number of visitors thinned, then finally stopped altogether. Dad was left alone.

My husband, Dick, and I asked Dad to come live with us on our small farm. We hoped the fresh air and rustic atmosphere would help him adjust.

Within a week after he moved in, I regretted the invitation. It seemed nothing was satisfactory. He criticized everything I did. I became frustrated and moody. Soon I was taking my pent-up anger out on Dick. We began to bicker and argue.

Alarmed, Dick sought out our pastor and explained the situation. The clergyman set up weekly counseling appointments for us. At the close of each session he prayed, asking God to soothe Dad's troubled mind.

But the months wore on and God was silent. Something had to be done and it was up to me to do it.

The next day I sat down with the phone book and methodically called each of the mental health clinics listed in the Yellow Pages. 1 explained my problem to each of the sympathetic voices that answered in vain.Just when I was giving up hope, one of the voices suddenly exclaimed, "I just read something that might help you! Let me go get the article."

I listened as she read. The article described a remarkable study done at a nursing home. All of the patients were under treatment for chronic depression. Yet their attitudes had improved dramatically when they were given responsibility for a dog.

I drove to the animal shelter that afternoon. After I filled out a questionnaire, a uniformed officer led me to the kennels. The odor of disinfectant stung my nostrils as I moved down the row of pens. Each contained five to seven dogs. Long-haired dogs, curly-haired dogs, black dogs, spotted dogs all jumped up, trying to reach me. I studied each one but rejected one after the other for various reasons too big, too small, too much hair. As I neared the last pen a dog in the shadows of the far corner struggled to his feet, walked to the front of the run and sat down. It was a pointer, one of the dog world's aristocrats. But this was a caricature of the breed.

Years had etched his face and muzzle with shades of gray. His hip bones jutted out in lopsided triangles. But it was his eyes that caught and held my attention. Calm and clear, they beheld me unwaveringly.

I pointed to the dog. "Can you tell me about him?" The officer looked, then shook his head in puzzlement. "He's a funny one. Appeared out of nowhere and sat in front of the gate. We brought him in, figuring someone would be right down to claim him. That was two weeks a~o and we've heard nothing. His time is up tomorrow." He gestured helplessly.

As the words sank in I turned to the man in horror. "You mean you're going to kill him?"

"Ma'am," he said gently, "that's our policy. We don't have room for every unclaimed dog."

I looked at the pointer again. The calm brown eyes awaited my decision. "I'll take him," I said. I drove home with the dog on the front seat beside me. When I reached the house I honked the horn twice. I was helping my prize out of the car when Dad shuffled onto the front porch... "Ta-da! Look what I got for you, Dad !" I said excitedly.

Dad looked, then wrinkled his face in disgust. "If I had wanted a dog I would have gotten one. And I would have picked out a

better specimen than that bag of bones. Keep it! I don't want it"
Dad waved his arm scornfully and turned back toward the house.

Anger rose inside me. It squeezed together my throat muscles
and pounded into my temples. "You'd better get used to him, Dad.
He's staying!"

Dad ignored me. "Did you hear me, Dad ?" I screamed. At
those words Dad whirled angrily, his hands clenched at his sides,
his eyes narrowed and blazing with hate. We stood glaring at each
other like duelists, when suddenly the pointer pulled free from my
grasp. He wobbled toward my dad and sat down in front of him.
Then slowly, carefully, he raised his paw.

Dad's lower jaw trembled as he stared at the uplifted paw
Confusion replaced the anger in his eyes. The pointer waited
patiently. Then Dad was on his knees hugging the animal.

It was the beginning of a warm and intimate friendship. Dad
named the pointer Cheyenne. Together he and Cheyenne explored
the community. They spent long hours walking down dusty lanes.
They spent reflective moments on the banks of streams, angling for
tasty trout. They even started to attend Sunday services together,
Dad sitting in a pew and Cheyenne lying quietly at is feet.

Dad and Cheyenne were inseparable throughout the next three
years. Dad's bitterness faded, and he and Cheyenne made many
friends. Then late one night I was startled to feel Cheyenne's cold
nose burrowing through our bed covers. He had never before come
into our bedroom at night. I woke Dick, put on my robe and ran
into my father's room. Dad lay in his bed, his face serene. But his
spirit had left quietly sometime during the night.

Two days later my shock and grief deepened when I discovered
Cheyenne lying dead beside Dad's bed. I wrapped his still form in
the rag rug he had slept on. As Dick and I buried him near a favorite
fishing hole, I silently thanked the dog for the help he had given
me in restoring Dad's peace of mind.

The morning of Dad's funeral dawned overcast and dreary. This day looks like the way I feel, I thought, as I walked down the aisle to the pews reserved for family. I was surprised to see the many friends Dad and Cheyenne had made filling the church. The pastor began his eulogy. It was a tribute to both Dad and the dog who had changed his life.And then the pastor turned to Hebrews 13:2. "Do not neglect to show hospitality to strangers, for by this some have entertained angels without knowing it."

"I've often thanked God for sending that angel," he said.

For me, the past dropped into place, completing a puzzle that I had not seen before: the sympathetic voice that had just read the right article... Cheyenne's unexpected appearance at the animal shelter. his calm acceptance and complete devotion to my father. hid the proximity of their deaths. And suddenly I understood. I knew that God had answered my prayers after ~i.

Life is too short for drama or petty things, so laugh hard, love tryky arid forgive quickly. Live While You Are Alive. Forgive now those who made you cry. You might not get a second time.

John 15:17 "If you abide in Me and My word abides in you, you will ask whatever you desire and it shall be done unto you."

A little child will lead us

The following are illustrations based on that thought
Bro Owens
Remember, you were once eight years old

" **P** lease remain standing for a word of pray as we dismiss."

Nothing was stated audible, but the sincere thought was there, "Please, don't call on Brother Owens. It's already late, if they get him started, he never knows when to quit."

Rev. Robinson called, "Brother Owens, will you close us with prayer?"

"Oh no, anything or anyone but him, we'll be here all night, he never knows when to quit, never. I wonder if he ever prays anywhere else or if he saves it all for Church, especially during revival meetings?"

Semi-annual revival meetings were regular as clockwork at the small Church, one in late spring and another in the fall or winter. This one was the later one; it was decided on months ago. As usual, there was no option, I would attend, we would attend, and all of us, there were six of us still at home. Don't know how the others felt, but it was Tuesday night and I had homework to do, that didn't matter, we would be in Church.

The congregation was generally made up of just a few families; there was our family, Dad was the Pastor of the local Church. Counting Rev. Robinson, the Evangelist and Mom and Dad, there were eight of us, enough to make a difference. John was the Song Leader, I never did know if he liked it or if it was one of those things he did because Dad said so.

Then the Wade's, they were some kind of relative on Mom's side of the family, which made five more. Mr. and Mrs. Miller, a pillar of the community, at least, a pillar of the Church. Mrs. Miller was the Pianist. The Burleson's were probably Mom and Dad's closest friends, until Mrs. Burleson's death at the hands of a drunk hit and run driver. At one time, Mr. Burleson grew a mustache, but shaved it off when too many people made fun of him. Never did really understand Mr. Hirschman, no one could depend on him for much. Last but not least, Mr. And Mrs. Owens, it was hard not to think of him as a bowling pin with legs.

The Church met in a Union Hall; a dark red brick building set in the middle of a residential area. I don't know if a Union still meets there. Actually, the Church was a Mission sat in North Alton, it was started by the Calvary Baptist Church also in Alton. On an average Sunday there may be thirty five in attendance with a good attendance may reach up to about fifty. This was the second week of a two week revival meeting, it snowed last night and there was freezing rain today. The crowd of twenty-two was pretty good considering everything.

Last Sunday, we had to go to dinner with the visiting preacher at some one's house that I didn't know I'm not sure anyone knew them. Even with fried chicken and ice cream, I would rather have been at home, but that wasn't an option. "One of these day when I'm older, I'm not going to go anywhere I don't want to go."

"My Gosh, is he still praying? Maybe he'll finish soon. It's not bad enough that the preacher preached too long, and we sang all the verses of "Just as I am" and then started over, it's late and he's still going, wish he'd shut up."

The Junior class always sat together, nothing said they had to, it was just customary. Not only that, but Mom wouldn't allow any of her boys to sit on the back row so they sat in the second row from the back. That wasn't OK, but was acceptable.

"I wish I was at home, I have home work that needs to be done, that would be better than being here. Gosh, he's still at it, does he ever stop?"

"Never noticed that light before, it blinks like crazy. He's still at it. Wonder what John's thinking? I'll bet he feels the same as I do. At least he's sitting by Virginia."

"I know it's been at least an hour, maybe longer, doesn't he ever run down? Even Mrs. Owens has to be tired of listening to him. At least he's asking for blessings for all of the Missionaries that mean he's about to stop. Next he'll be praying about the ungodly country and praying for our politicians to straighten up and do the right thing. It's always the same thing. He should just print it and we can all read it and go home, it's always the same thing,"

"If it was summer it would still be dark, maybe we'll have a decent softball team next summer. Wonder how Tom Mix will find his way off that mountain in the blizzard. Hope I win that bike they're giving away."

"Wow, even Mom is starting to fidget, she'll fuss about it on the way home. Even she can only take so much."

"He's still at it. Do you suppose God gets tired of listening to the same thing over and over?"

Out of the mouths of babes!

What does "Love" mean to you? Children

When my grandmother got arthritis, she couldn't bend over and paint her toenails anymore. So my grandfather does it for her all the time, even when his hands got arthritis too. That's Love" – Rebecca – age 8

When someone loves you, the way they say your name is different. You just know that your name is safe in their mouth – Billy – age 4

Love is when a girl puts on perfume and a boy puts on shaving cologne and they go out and smell each other – Karl – age 5

Love is when you go out to eat and give somebody most of your French fries without making them give you any of theirs. – Chrissy – age 6

Love is what makes you smile when you're tired – Terri age 4

Love is when my mommy makes coffee for my daddy and she takes a sip before giving it to him to make sure the taste is OK. – Danny – age 7

Love is when you kiss all the time. Then when you get tired of kissing, you still want to be together and talk more. My Mommy and Daddy are like that. They look gross when they kiss. – Emily – age 8

Love is what's in the room with you at Christmas if you stop opening presents and listen – Bobby age 7 (WOW)

If you want to learn to love better, you should start with a friend who you hate – Nikka – age 6

Love is when you tell a guy you like his shirt, then he wears it everyday – Noelle – age 7

Love is like a little old woman and a little old man who are still friends even after they know each other so well Tommy – age 8

During my piano recital, I was on a stage and I was scared. I looked at all the people watching me and saw my daddy waving and smiling. – He was the only one doing that. I wasn't scared anymore – Cindy – age 8

My mommy loves me more that anybody. You don't see anyone else kissing me to sleep at night – Clare – age 6

Love is when Mommy gives Daddy the best piece of chicken, Elaine – age 5

Dear God.

Instead of letting people die and having to make new ones, why don't you just keep the ones you got now?"

Jane

Dear God,

In Bible time, did people really talk like the"

Jennifer

Dear God

Please put another holiday between Christmas and Easter, there isn't any there now"

Ginny

Dear God,

"We read that Thomas Edison made the light, our Sunday School teachers said You did. I'll bet he stole the idea from you."

Donna

When there is nothing left but God that is when you find out that God is all you need

Kids will be kids

A perfect Sunday morning. A gentle breeze nestled the lone tree near the sanctuary, in t he distance, a lone bird could be heard, all's well with the world.

The Worship was well attended as was usual, It was obvious the Preacher was preparing to approach the pulpit, the congregation was completing the third verse of "What a fried we have in Jesus:

Five year old Dan tugged on the tail of his mother's coat, loudly announcing, "did you notice how Miss Simmons sure is stupid." As he pointed toward a spot a couple of pews in front of them, those seated nearby gently laughed except mom who was busy berating Dan

His announcement was closely followed by,

"Be quiet, shame on you for saying anything like that."

"But Mom, she is, just look at her.:

Mom and Dan quickly proceeded to leave the service and not very quietly as Mom addressee the boy, "I told you to be quiet."

"But Mom, look at her, see the way she's bent over.

Some of those in the area heard Mom's comments, others were too busy laughing, she isn't stupid, she has arthritis she just can't stand straight like most people, she isn't stupid"

A child was asked to write a book report on the entire Bible. Here is what he wrote;

The Children's Bible in a Nutshell

In the beginning, which occurred near the start, there was nothing but God, darkness, and some gas. The Bible says," The Lord thy God is one," but I think He must be a lot older than that.

Anyway, God said, "Give me a light!" and someone did.

Then God made the world.

He split the Adam and made Eve. Adam and Eve were naked, but they weren't embarrassed because mirrors hadn't been invented yet.

Adam and Eve disobeyed God by eating one bad apple, so they were driven from the Garden of Eden. . . . . Not sure what they were driven in though, because they didn't have cars.

Adam and Eve had a son, Cain, who hated his brother as long as he was Abel.

Pretty soon all of the early people died off, except for Methuselah, who lived to be like a million or something.

One of the next important people was Noah, who was a good guy, but one of his kids was kind of a Ham. Noah built a large boat and put his family and some animals on it. He asked some other people to join him, but they said they would have to take a rain check.

After Noah came Abraham, Isaac, and Jacob. Jacob was more famous than his brother, Esau, because Esau sold Jacob his birthmark in exchange for some pot roast. Jacob had a son named Joseph who wore a really loud sports coat.

Another important Bible guy is Moses, whose real name was Charlton Heston. Moses led the Israel Lights out of Egypt and away from the evil Pharaoh after God sent ten plagues on Pharaoh's people. These plagues included frogs, mice, lice, bowels, and no cable.

God fed the Israel Lights every day with manicotti. Then he gave them His Top Ten Commandments. These include: don't lie, cheat, smoke, dance, or covet your neighbor's stuff.

Oh, yeah, I just thought of one more: Humor thy father and thy mother.

One of Moses' best helpers was Joshua who was the first Bible guy to use spies. Joshua fought the battle of Geritol and the fence fell over on the town.

After Joshua came David. He got to be king by killing a giant with a slingshot. He had a son named Solomon who had about 300 wives and 500 porcupines. My teacher says he was wise, but that doesn't sound very wise to me.

After Solomon there were a bunch of major league prophets. One of these was Jonah, who was swallowed by a big whale and then barfed up on the shore. There were also some minor league prophets, but I guess we don't have to worry about them.

After the Old Testament came the New Testament. Jesus is the star of The New Testament. He was born in Bethlehem in a barn. (I wish I had been born in a barn too, because my mom is always saying to me, "Close the door! Were you born in a barn?" It would be nice to say, "As a matter of fact, I was.")

During His life, Jesus had many arguments with sinners like the Pharisees and the Republicans.

Jesus also had twelve opossums. The worst one was Judas Asparagus. Judas was so evil that they named a terrible vegetable after him.

Jesus was a great man. He healed many leopards and even preached to some Germans on the Mount.

But the Democrats and all those guys put Jesus on trial before Pontius the Pilot. Pilot didn't stick up for Jesus. He just washed his hands instead.

Anyways, Jesus died for our sins, then came back to life again. He went up to Heaven but will be back at the end of the Aluminum. His return is foretold in the book of Revolution.

Matthew 26:41–Watch and pray that you enter not into temptation ...

This is include for grins

Good bye Angel, hello Satan

F amiliar and annoying scratching at the front door interrupted a restful Saturday afternoon resting, taking a much needed nap; it had been a long week. He knew the source of the noise, he also knew if it wasn't addressed the irritation would continue. Source of the noise? The cat, he hated that cat, as well as most cats.

Gregory didn't like the cat; in fact, he hated it. The worse part of the whole event was that his wife Hilda loved Satan, a large solid black pedigreed Angora cat. A perfect name for any cat and especially this one. If he tried, he could say it was pretty. He didn't try.

Loud scratching and screaming at the front door was in keeping with history for the cat. Hilda was gone for the weekend visiting her sister in Paducah; she won't be back until Monday. It's a perfect time to solve the problem, "I've a perfect plan."

In short order, Satan found himself reluctantly screaming and scratching in the trunk of the old Chevy, Greg was happy and satisfied, his problem, at least that one would soon be over. They were on the way to an area near where he grew up, a place miles from anywhere. An ideal area, with any luck, a wild animal would finish Satan but that wasn't Greg's problem, the cat would have to fend for himself. They arrived at the destination within about a half of an hour. A nice wooden place covered with trees and other shrubs, there was no one anywhere around for a long way. No one would ever know. Though he didn't like the cat, he didn't think it proper and right to kill it, he would just dump it and leave.

The trunk lid was opened. Once again, the cat screamed, jumped and was last seen disappearing into the woods. Good, that was easy and is now over; I won't have to worry about this again. Smiling and happy, a leisurely ride home and a reflection on a job well done. A few minutes later the car rested in the driveway, a few steps to the front door, there was Satan, as big and black as ever and as angry, hissing and screaming. He told himself, that can't be, I left him miles away and there is no way he could get here before me. That may be true, but there he was.

The door was opened, the cat got in before Greg. The first thought, at least I won't have to explain what happen to the cat when Hilda returns on Monday. "I'll just have to get over it and forget.

There was still time to complete the nap, he just settled down on the living room couch. A gentle rap on the front door, he wasn't sure he heard it but decided he was mistaken; the sound was loud enough to interrupt his rest. The knock was louder this time; no doubt there was someone there. It was the elderly next door neighbor Miss Simmons, "Have you seen Angel?"

"NO! Who is Angel?"

"My cat, I let her out a couple of hours ago and haven't seen her since. That's not like her to hide or be gone so long."

"I'm not sure I've ever seen your cat, what kind of cat?"

"Angel is a large, beautiful, black angora cat about six years old."

Now he knew how Satan arrived home first, it wasn't Satan that he dropped off in the woods, it was Angel. "No, I'm sure I've never seen your cat, I don't think I've ever seen it, if I do, I'll let you know."

Miss Simmons turned and left the porch, muttering. "This is so unlike Angel, I hope she comes home soon."

CPSIA information can be obtained
at www.ICGtesting.com
Printed in the USA
LVHW010620090720
660121LV00011BC/1127